KU-136-803

James and Chantal live in a small town near Cannes, in France. This afternoon they are in their garden. James is looking at the newspaper.

'Where can we go this evening?' Chantal asks.

'Let's go to the Blue **Cat Club**,' James says. 'It's very good. Look! You can eat and drink. And you can dance. We can drive there.'

They drive down into Cannes and look for the Blue Cat Club. It is in a big street near the sea.

'Oh, look,' Chantal says. 'There it is. And look! There's a **cabaret**, too. Merlin, Man of **Magic**. Good. I love magic.'

cat /kæt/ (n) The *cat* plays in the garden and sleeps in the house.
club /klʌb/ (n) I want to dance. Let's go to a *club*!
cabaret /ˈkæbəreɪ/ (n) We can eat first and then watch the *cabaret*.
magic /ˈmædʒɪk/ (n) The pen is on the table – and now it isn't. Is that *magic*?

ub

5|7   CLS

CO IN BACK

CENTRAL LIBRARY

- 2 MAR 2008

2 - DEC 2010

WITHDRAWN FROM ROTHERHAM PUBLIC LIBRARY

ROTHERHAM LIBRARY & INFORMATION SERVICES

This book must be returned by the date specified at the time of issue
as the DATE DUE FOR RETURN.
The loan may be extended (personally, by post or telephone) for a
further period if the book is not required by another reader, by quoting
the above number / author / title.

LIS7a

Potter

1.1 What's the book about?

Look at the pictures on the front of this book and on pages 1 and 2.

1 Talk about them. What can you see?

2 Tick (✓) the right answers.

    a What is the Blue Cat Club?

        a football club ☐   a school club ☐

        a nightclub ☐   a film club ☐

    b What does a 'Man of Magic' do?

3 **The young man and the young woman on page 1 are James and Chantal. Circle the right words in the sentences.**

    a Chantal is *young* / *old* and her hair is *long* / *short*.

    b James and Chantal live in a *small* / *big* house near the *sea* / *town*.

    c They see the name of a *cinema* / *club* in a *newspaper* / *book*.

1.2 What happens first?

What do you think? Are the sentences right (✓) or wrong (✗)?

1 Chantal loves magic. ◯

2 They go into Cannes in their car. ◯

3 The club is the Black Cat Club. ◯

4 There is a man of magic at the club. ◯

5 You can't dance at the club. ◯

6 James has a good time there. ◯

'OK,' James says. 'Let's go in and get a good table at the **front**.'

They go into the Blue Cat Club and sit at a table at the front. There is music and people are dancing. James asks a man for some drinks.

'It's a hot night. A **tomato juice**, please,' he says. 'And for you, Chantal?'

'A tomato juice for me, too, please,' she says.

The man brings the drinks quickly to their table.

front /frʌnt/ (n) Our garden is at the *front* of the house.
tomato juice /tə'mɑːtəʊ dʒuːs/ (n) She only drinks water or *tomato juice*.

Suddenly the music stops
and the cabaret starts. They
see Merlin, the Man of Magic.
He is very clever. He walks from table to table. He goes behind
the people at the tables. He is very friendly. He takes fruit from a
woman's hair and an **egg** from a man's mouth. People are **laugh**ing.
Chantal loves it.

egg /eg/ (n) I have two *eggs* every morning before school.
laugh /lɑːf/ (v) I am a bad dancer. People *laugh* at me.

'How does he do that?' she says to James.

Now Merlin is standing behind James and Chantal.

'Good evening,' he smiles. 'Who is this beautiful girl? And that's a beautiful dress, too.'

He **touch**es Chantal's hair, and her dress. He touches James's **shoulder**, too.

James is unhappy. The man is very friendly and James does not like it.

touch /tʌtʃ/ (v) Please don't *touch* the picture!
shoulder /ˈʃəʊldə/ (n) The child is sitting on his father's *shoulders*.

'And now,' Merlin says with a smile, 'what have I got here for this beautiful girl? A **necklace**!'

'Oh, my necklace!' Chantal says. 'Look, James! He's got my necklace.'

Merlin smiles and gives her the necklace.

He smiles at James, too. But James is very quiet. People are laughing and he is not happy.

necklace /ˈnekləs/ (n) That is a beautiful *necklace*!

'Oh, look at this young man.' Merlin smiles. 'He isn't very happy. Look at his face. He's angry with me. And why is he angry? Look! I have his money and ... his **watch**.'

Merlin has James's watch and his **wallet** in his hands.

'Here you are.' He smiles. 'One watch and one wallet. It's only my little game.'

watch /wɒtʃ/ (n) What time is it? Have you got a *watch*?
wallet /ˈwɒlət/ (n) Is there any money in your *wallet*?

2.1 Were you right?

Look at your answers to Activity 1.2 on page ii. Then finish the sentences.

1 Chantal loves ....*magic*............. .

2 They go into Cannes in their ....

3 The club is the .... Cat Club.

4 Merlin is a man of ....

5 You .... dance at the club.

6 James .... a good time there.

2.2 What more did you learn?

Finish the sentences with words from the boxes.

1 Chantal's dress is ....*long*.......... and ....*beautiful*.......... .

long	old	beautiful	short

2 James is .... and ....

tall	fat	young	short

3 Merlin is .... and ....

angry	clever	young	friendly

4 Merlin touches Chantal's .... and ....

hair	foot	hand	dress

5 Merlin takes James's .... and ....

egg	watch	necklace	wallet

6 On page 7 James is .... and ....

hot	angry	quiet	happy

2.3 ## Language in use

Look at the sentence on the right. Then
look at the pictures. Put the words from
the box into the sentences.

> James and Chantal live **in** a
> small town **near** Cannes.

with	under	in front of	in	from	behind	on	near

1 James is .... the club .... Chantal.

2 The drinks are .... the table .... them.

3 Merlin is standing .... James and Chantal.

4 He's taking James's wallet .... his coat.

5 There is a bag .... the table .... Chantal's
foot.

2.4 ## What's next?

Two men bring a big box on to the stage. What does Merlin do with it?
What does he think? Write *Yes* or *No*.

1 A person goes into the box.   ....

2 Merlin goes into the box.   ....

3 Chantal goes into the box.   ....

4 James goes into the box.   ....

5 The five swords go into the box.   ....

Now two men bring a big, heavy **box** on to the **stage**. There are five **hole**s in the front of the box and five long **sword**s in the holes. You can see the **end**s of the swords behind the box.

Merlin takes the five swords out of the holes and opens the door of the box.

'And now,' he says, 'I want one **volunteer**, please.'

box /bɒks/ (n) My letters are in a *box* under my bed.
stage /steɪdʒ/ (n) I can't stand on a *stage* and talk to people.
hole /həʊl/ (n) Look! There is a *hole* in your shirt.
sword /sɔːd/ (n) He always has a *sword* in his hand in the film.
end /end/ (n) Do you know the *end* of the story?
volunteer /ˌvɒlənˈtɪə/ (n) He does interesting work but he is a *volunteer*.

Merlin looks at Chantal with a smile.

'Perhaps you can be my volunteer,' he says.

James stands up quickly. He puts his hands on Chantal's shoulders.

'No,' he says. 'Not her, thank you.'

'Then perhaps *you*, young man.' Merlin smiles. 'You can come and stand in my box. It's not difficult.'

James stands at the table. What can he do? The people in the room are looking at him. They are waiting.

Chantal is looking at him, too.

'You can do it,' she says quietly. 'It's only magic. Go on the stage and get in the box for him.'

'OK,' James says slowly.

He goes on to the stage and gets into the big box.

Now James is in the box. Merlin closes the door at the front. He smiles at the people in the room. He takes one of the swords and **push**es it slowly into a hole in the door of the box.

The people in the room are very quiet. Is the young man in the box OK? Merlin pushes swords two, three and four into the box, too.

push /pʊʃ/ (v) *Push* the door open!

3.1 Right or wrong?

Look at your answers to Activity 2.4 on page 9. Then tick (✓) the right answers to this question.

Who/What goes into Merlin's box?

3.2 What more did you learn?

What comes first? And then? Write the numbers, 1–8.

A Merlin opens the door of the box.

B James puts his hands on Chantal's shoulders.

C Two men bring a big box on to the stage. `1`

D Merlin asks for a volunteer.

E Merlin closes the door of the box.

F Merlin takes the swords out of the holes in the box.

G James goes into the box.

H Merlin pushes the swords into the holes in the box.

3.3 Language in use

Look at the sentence on the right. Can you do it? Write *Yes, I can* or *No, I can't*.

> 'You can do it,' she said quietly.

1 James can read English books. Can you? ....Yes, I can.........

2 James can swim. Can you? ....

3 Chantal can drive a car. Can you? ....

4 James and Chantal can dance. Can you? ....

5 James can run very quickly. Can you? ....

6 Chantal can take good photos. Can you? ....

7 James can play football well. Can you? ....

8 James can understand Japanese. Can you? ....

9 James can stand on one leg. Can you? ....

10 Chantal can't do magic. Can you? ....

3.4 What's next?

What do you think? Write the names.

At the end of the story:

1 Who is happy? ....

2 Who is angry? ....

3 Who is laughing? ....

Merlin has only one sword now. There is only one hole in the door. Merlin smiles again at the people in front of him, and pushes the sword in quickly.

'Aaaaaagh!'

Merlin smiles at the people at the tables in front of him.

'Perhaps the young man is having a little game with us,' he says. But he looks very unhappy.

Merlin takes the swords quickly from the box. One, two, three, four, five, all on the floor of the stage.

Slowly he opens the door of the box.

James is in it but he is not moving. His eyes are closed. His shirt under his hands is red – very red.

'Oh, no!' Merlin says. 'What's wrong? I don't understand. I ... I'm sorry!'

17

Suddenly James opens his eyes. He smiles at Merlin. In his hands he has a small bottle.

'It's OK,' he laughs. 'It's only tomato juice. It's only my little game, Mr Magic.'

Merlin's face is very red now. The people at the tables are laughing at him. He goes away quickly. The music starts again and people dance.

James goes to Chantal and sits down at the table again. He puts the bottle of tomato juice on the table and smiles at her.

'Only my little game,' he says again quietly.

She takes his hand.

'Don't be angry.' She smiles at him. 'You're always *my* Mr Magic ... always.'

1 **Who thinks these words? When in the story? Why?**

a 'Let's play a game with this man. Where's that bottle of tomato juice?'

b 'This is a beautiful young woman. Let's put her in the box.'

c 'He's very clever. How can he take her necklace? Oh, and my wallet too.'

d 'Oh no! He's dead. What can I do?'

e 'This is bad. James is angry now. It's only magic. It isn't important.'

2 **Work with a friend.**

| Student A: | You are Merlin, the Man of Magic. You have your big box on the stage and now you want a volunteer for your magic. Ask Student B. You don't want his/her friends. |
| Student B: | You are visiting the club with some friends. You are sitting quietly at your table and you are happy there. Perhaps one of your friends can be the volunteer. |

Write about it

Write about the Blue Cat Club for an English language newspaper in Cannes.

New Club in Town!

The Blue ....Cat....... Club is a .... nightclub in Cannes. It opens this week. It is .... every evening from 7 to 12 o'clock. You can have good .... and drink there in a big, beautiful .... There is .... every evening and you can dance. There is a .... every evening too. This week it is a famous Man of .... His .... is Merlin. He is very clever. He takes a .... from the people in the club and puts him into a big .... on the .... Then he pushes five long swords into .... in the box. Then the person comes out again. It is all very clever. .... does he do it? Go to the club and watch him.

1 You and your friends are making a film. One student is a Man of Magic or a Woman of Magic. He or she does the magic. Three or four students are in the club. They can watch and be volunteers.

Talk about the questions.

a What magic can you do? Write six things. Then choose one. How can you put it on film?

1 ......*Push swords into a person in a box.*......

2 ....

3 ....

4 ....

5 ....

6 ....

b Where can you make this film?

c What do you want for it? (A table, a box ...)

2 **Write the story for your film.**

Story	Words
• The Man of Magic talks to the people in the club. He wants a volunteer for his magic. • He asks a man but the man goes under his table. The woman with him is angry ...	• Man of Magic: 'Good evening. Can I have a volunteer, please? You – can you come on the stage, please?' • Man: 'No – no, thank you.' ...

Story	Words
....	....
....	....
....	....
....	....
....	....
....	
....	
....	
....	
....	
....	
....	

3 **Make a poster for your film.**

- What is the name of the film?
- Who is in it?
- What is in the picture?
- Where can people see the film?
- When can they see it?